The Book Enchained

THE BOOK ENCHAINED

HARRISON E. SALISBURY

a lecture sponsored by the Center for the Book in the Library of Congress and the Authors League of America

presented at the Library of Congress September 28, 1983

LIBRARY OF CONGRESS Washington 1984

The Center for the Book
Viewpoint Series
No. 10

Library of Congress Cataloging in Publication Data

Salisbury, Harrison Evans, 1908–
The book enchained.

(The Center for the Book viewpoint series ; 10)
Supt. of Docs. no.: LC 1.38:10
"A lecture sponsored by The Center for the Book in the Library of Congress and the Authors League of America; presented at the Library of Congress September 28, 1983."
1. Censorship—Addresses, essays, lectures.
2. Freedom of speech—Addresses, essays, lectures.
3. Books and reading—Addresses, essays, lectures.
I. Title. II. Series.
Z657.S16 1984 323.44'5 84-600006
ISBN 0-8444-0447-0

This booklet is printed on permanent/durable paper.

PREFACE

IS IT POSSIBLE THAT THE TRADITIONAL BOOK IS threatened in our "enlightened" age? Writer and historian Harrison E. Salisbury, for many years an editor and foreign correspondent for the *New York Times*, thinks so. His provocative lecture, "The Book Enchained," was presented at the Library of Congress on September 28, 1983, under the joint sponsorship of the Center for the Book in the Library of Congress and the Authors League of America. The lecture was presented in memory of Luise Marie Sillcox, executive secretary of the Authors League of America, who served the league and the writers of this country for nearly half a century. Barbara Tuchman's Sillcox lecture, presented in 1979, was the first publication in the Center for the Book's Viewpoint Series. The center is now pleased to publish Mr. Salisbury's talk, the second Sillcox lecture, as Viewpoint No. 10.

Proposed by Librarian of Congress Daniel J. Boorstin and established by an Act of Congress in 1977, the Center for the Book exists to keep the book flourishing by stimulating interest in books, reading, and the printed word. The center works closely with organizations outside the Library of Congress to promote reading, to address contemporary issues related to books and the printed word, and to encourage the study of the history of books. It pursues these goals primarily by bringing together members of the book, educational, and business communities for symposia and projects. It also sponsors lectures, visiting scholars, exhibits, publications, and events that enhance the role of the book in our society.

The Center for the Book's activities are supported by tax-deductible contributions from individuals and organizations. This publication would not be possible without such support from Mrs. Charles W. Engelhard, to whom we are grateful.

John Y. Cole
Executive Director
The Center for the Book

We have assembled tonight in a citadel of human knowledge such as the world has never seen, greater than those of Alexandria, of Carthage, of Imperial Peking or than the vast repositories of London, Paris, and Rome. It stands, I think, at the peak of civilization, of man's ability to create, to learn, to penetrate the mysteries of the universe and of the human mind. Within these precincts one must speak with care—eons are listening.

Fifty years ago as a young newspaperman I used to walk into the beautiful old Library of Congress (which for me is and always will be *the* library) and work for hours and days in the great reading room, sending in my slips for books and waiting for their arrival. In that time it never occurred to me that I was working within the nucleus of a miracle. To me there seemed nothing unusual about walking in from the street and ordering up any book that had been published since Gutenberg with no more identification than my name and address. That, I thought, was the way all libraries worked; that was the natural relationship of reader to book—free, universal, no questions asked.

I have learned better since. The book, I now know, is an exquisite example of human genius. Where it flourishes, man flourishes. Where it withers, humanity withers. The book is strong. It can endure for a thousand years and more, but there exist those who would put out its eyes, black its words, reduce it to a gray heap of ashes, lock it in chains, and let generations live and die in darkness. Nor are those enemies of the book to be found only in strange and evil lands beyond the oceans. The enemies of the book are here among us in this great land of ours, even in Washington, this most free of capitals—those who would confine books again with medieval locks, tear them from the library shelves, ban their use by scholars, students, and ordinary citizens, seal up the vaults of human knowledge and stamp it "Top Secret." Oh, yes, the white-jacketed priests of the Security Cult, the Know-Nothings, the Yahoos, the Galloots are never far distant. Even as we await the dawn of the twenty-first century they are with us, smudging the texts of Aristotle and Plato, wiping filthy noses with the scripts of Einstein and Oppenheimer, and pawing through Mark Twain, William Faulkner, Ernest Hemingway, and William Styron for passages which can be distorted into "threats" to the innocence of the young.

The signs on the library reading rooms may proclaim silence, but monastic calm is seldom found in the world of the book. Nor has it been since Socrates sought to demonstrate to his peers that what they had taken for knowledge was, in fact, ignorance. This misperception among eminent men is not unknown today. We may solace ourselves with the thought that the world remembers Socrates but long since has forgotten the poet Meletus, the tanner Anytus, and the orator Lycon, who brought the charges that Socrates was guilty of denying the gods recognized by the state and introducing new divinities and, also, that he was corrupting the young. Under names equally banal the descendents of Meletus, Anytus, and Lycon are among us still, ready and eager to raise the mob against the man who dares proclaim that the Emperor stands naked, and not, as he insists, clothed in royal purple.

It is well to recall that fifty years ago in Germany, that great country which was the pride of Europe, seat of ancient universities and the most advanced scientific knowledge, birthplace of Heine, Goethe, Schiller, and Thomas Mann, of Mozart, Bach, and Beethoven—Germany, where knowledge and its pursuit was venerated above all, where the highest of all titles was "Herr Doctor Professor"—in that gentle Germany books were set afire in the streets, artists and scholars, poets, and philosophers were dragged into cattle cars, yellow armbands affixed to their sleeves; bound for destinations from which they would never return. All this occurred in a land where the passion for order was so profound that jokesters said Germany could never have a revolution because no German would disobey the injunction "Do Not Walk on the Grass."

Alas, that German temple of humanity, that shrine to the book and to a humane life was blown away by the ranting of a second-rate artist, a man who fashioned hatred, anger, frustration, xenophobia, and ignorance into a strident doctrine which turned a decent people into a Hunnish mob.

We can and should pride ourselves on our freedom of expression and on the Bill of Rights which is the foundation of the freedom of the book, of thought, and of expression. But let us remember that no Bill of Rights, no constitutional privilege is stronger than the comity of the society which exists under that Bill of Rights and that Constitution. Courts, as Mr. Dooley said so long ago, follow the election returns. If in America today there exists a majority—or even a well-organized minority—which would not sign the Declaration of Independence—and sees no need for a Bill of Rights—watch out! The enemy is within our doors.

Unless we rise in defense of our traditions, rights, and liberties, the doomsday of George Orwell's *1984* may be as close at hand as the calendar suggests. It is no longer unimaginable that by shouting loud enough a clever ruler can make Liberty mean Slavery, War mean Peace (already we hear nuclear weapons being called "peace-keepers"), and Ignorance be paraded as Knowledge.

There are three great enemies of the book. The first is fire, which (sometimes combined with war) robbed successive civilizations of great heritages. In the present day the hazard of fire can be well guarded against, but it is important to remember that this very congressional library twice was devastated by flames, first in 1814, by fire set by the British, and then in 1851, when the blaze left only twenty thousand volumes on the blackened shelves.

The other dangers are more difficult to ward off. War takes a toll not only of life but of the heritage of life which is the book. In this nuclear age, war means not only the total destruction of humanity but the obliteration of man's knowledge and achievements, the Rosetta stones on which a future might be postulated. It will all go.

Then there is tyranny. Tyranny has ever been and is today the enemy of the book and of man himself. Hate, distrust, fear, insecurity—these are the handmaidens of tyranny and the enemies of the book. Instinctively men hate and fear what they do not know and do not understand. In this late twentieth-century decade many Americans hate and fear the Soviet Union. Some call it an "evil empire," a black kingdom which threatens the bright new world, that city on a hill which we believe we have created.

Well, there are and have been dark forces in Russia—and you will note that I make a distinction between Russia and the Soviet Union, a very important distinction and one of which many Americans, including those in very high office, know little. These have existed for many centuries. Some are products of today's ideologies. Others are rooted deep in Russian history and culture. Aleksandr Solzhenitsyn has touched on this in a slightly different way, warning us not to confuse the Soviet regime with the traditional Russia. But that is another matter.

Russia did not experience the liberating influence of Renaissance and Reformation. Her revolution came nearly 150 years after the American Revolution, 125 years after that of the French, and 75 years after Europe's great stirrings of 1840. By 1914 Russia was finally rushing breakneck into the industrial revolution, but how much did she still lag behind the West—one century? Two, in some ways. Put today's Soviet system back into the seventeenth century—it would seem advanced in many ways. Match it against the post-industrial world, the information explosion, the jet-and-computer society, and it seems the kind of land in which our forefathers toiled—dark, dangerous, difficult.

No wonder. For three hundred years Mongol despots sat on Russia's back, and they were overthrown by Russian despots just as cruel and bloody. Ivan the Terrible did not win his title in Sunday school. His secret police and executioners were the direct ancestors of those of Stalin. The book came late to Russia and it came in chains. The imprisonment of the book by the Russian Orthodox church was total, perhaps no more total than that of the Roman church of the Inquisition and Index but displaced in time, persisting almost to contemporary days. Not until the seventeenth century did that contradictory man, Peter the Great, found the Imperial Library—with books he had seized in his conquest of Kurland. Catherine the Great, sometimes thought of as a liberal, granted the library its first great accession, 200,000 books of the fine Polish collection of Count Zaluski, seized in Warsaw and transported to St. Petersburg in 1795.

It seems hardly necessary to add that the magnificent imperial collection was never made freely available in the sense that collections of the British Museum or the Library of Congress were. Russia was then as the Soviet Union is today—a bastion of the official censor. The formal office of censor we owe to the Romans of 443 B.C. But the censor in one guise or another has never been far from the seat of power since the dawn of civilization, and he is alive and well in Washington today, presiding over a multitude of edicts restricting this, restricting that, labeling enormous warehouses of bureaucratic wastepaper with various security classifications.

But nowhere has the censor enjoyed a more active and ubiquitous life than in Russia. Nicholas I himself undertook to act as censor for the poet Pushkin, whom he professed to admire. Catherine the Great personally sent a rather second-rate poet to a madhouse when he deigned to write a hymn in praise of the American Revolution. The present Soviet regime was hardly the first to find the madhouse a convenient lodging place for inconvenient poets and writers. And as we condemn the practice, let us not forget our own sorry story of Ezra Pound and St. Elizabeth's. Of course it is now said the madhouse "protected" Pound from a worse fate. I wonder.

To this day, no great Russian writer has escaped the iron fist of the censor—Pushkin, Lermontov, Dostoyevsky, Gogol, Turgenev, Tolstoy, Chekhov, Gorky, Pasternak, and Solzhenitsyn. Only Karl Marx survived the halberd of Russia's Lord of Books. In what must have been a bemused mood, the imperial censor approved the publication of a Russian translation of *Das Kapital*, because, as he said, the exposition was so scientific and mathematic it could hardly be said to be popular.

Of the vagaries of the Russian censorship there is no end. In the 1880s the importation of sheet music from Germany was prohibited in the belief the musical notations might contain coded messages for revolutionaries. In the early years of the Soviet era, censors told foreign correspondents to use the mail or telephone to transmit abroad dispatches which the censor, charged only with supervision of cable traffic, could not clear.

There has been only one short uncertain span in Russia's constant effort to protect herself against the dangers of the book and the pen. This was the brief period between the Revolution of 1905 and that of 1917. It is only too expectable that Vladimir Lenin and his Bolsheviks campaigned for years against the censorship of the czars. But on the first day that Lenin came to power in October of 1917 he presented to the soviet the decree of censorship under which the Soviet Union still endures. Not only can no book be published in the Soviet Union without the approval of Glavlit, the Chief Office for Literary Affairs, as it is blandly called, but not one word can be printed, not even a matchbox cover, without the stamp of Glavlit.

And so, along with the censorship, the Soviet regime has continued and even improved upon the apparatus by which the Romanov state blinkered itself and walled itself off against progress and evolutionary development—the police, the prisons, the terror, inhumanity, injustice, arbitrary rule of power, the propaganda, and the diktat.

Small wonder that the lives of poets in the Soviet epoch make up a calendar written in blood—suicides, deaths by madness, deaths in charnel houses, deaths by attrition, and talents blighted by the Stalinist edict that writers must be the "engineers of human souls," whatever in the devil's name he could have meant by that. The tragic deaths of poets in the Soviet era are almost without end—Blok, Yesenin, Mayakovsky, Tsvetaeva, and Mandelshtam, to mention only a handful.

It is, I think, a tribute to Russian spirit and Russian

genius that despite this black record poetry lives on in the Soviet Union and that Evgeny Yevtushenko, Andrei Voznesensky, and Bella Akhmadulina still write and struggle for the free word and the free book. But it is a tragedy that Joseph Brodsky, probably the best living Russian poet, was expelled by the police from his native land over his violent protests (much as was Solzhenitsyn) and now lives and writes in America, our gain, Russia's loss.

Against this background it should surprise no one that the library in Russia is organized very much like the three circles of hell. The great Lenin library, a treasure-house of books that rivals the Library of Congress, is organized a bit like Fort Knox. The outer circle with the general catalog is available to recognized students and scholars possessed of requisite passports, certificates of identity, and papers certifying to their need and right to examine these books.

But, of course, the selection in the outer catalog is limited, especially in politically sensitive areas. The second circle is for more qualified scholars, those who are aspirants for a higher degree, those with special security clearance, those with party documentation.

The third circle is an inner citadel in which some restricted documents and books are available to those with senior credentials and high party and political validation. But within that are other circles, other catalogs, some of whose very existence is known only to the most trusted scholar-bureaucrats. What they contain no one on the outside can know for certain. Here, we presume, rest the surviving archives of Trotsky; here perhaps may be found the long suppressed writings of Bukharin, of Zinoviev, of Kamenev, of Radek, of the endless rolls of those once powerful, once annointed with power, now hurled into oblivion. Here is the memory hole of Soviet history (and of Russian history, as well). Here trespass is seldom granted. Great blocks of materials on the revolution itself, on the relations of Lenin with his party comrades or even with his family and friends, are known to be held in strictest secrecy. Here lie the deepest secrets of the Stalin era (if they have not long since been destroyed), the details of his endless murders, the minutiae of his paranoia, the last letter of denunciation from his wife Nadezhda before she took her own life, the bitter details of Stalin's mindless destruction of communist movements in other countries, the poisonous evidence of his intrigues with Hitler.

Who knows what other terrible tales lie hidden in these inner circles of hell, designated as libraries or archival deposits in the Soviet Union.

We all know the enemies of the book who flourish in this and other totalitarian states. The very existence of an ideological doctrine condemns dissident opinion to destruction or suppression.

It will, I fear, be some generations before one may reasonably expect to free the book of the fetters which enmesh it in the Soviet state. The process is not speeded, indeed, it is slowed, by every firestorm of tension or of outrage provoked by the kind of governmental conduct engendered when free inquiry is treated as blasphemy and treason.

What is to be done? That is the question which haunted the perplexed minds of Russia's nineteenth century. The answer was never found. Or rather a dozen answers were produced, none satisfactory. What is to be done by us? Surely, inescapably, our answer is clear. Do not follow the fateful path of tyranny and enchained truth. Strike down those bonds wherever and however they threaten the freedom of the American book and the American mind. Do not permit our own faceless bureaucrats to harass foreign poets seeking the traditional sanctuary of our great republic. Strike down the bony hands of our high priests of pseudo-security who would save the book by placing it within impregnable vaults. Let us take our stand with John Milton on the side of free ideas, a free intellect, and faith in the truth to conquer any false doctrine. For as Milton said: "Who kills a man kills a reasonable creature, God's image; but he who destroys a good book kills reason itself."

Let us conduct ourselves that no one may ever ask whether the Statue of Liberty still stands in New York harbor. If we follow this course not only will we protect and preserve our own freedom but the light of Liberty's torch slowly but surely will penetrate all corners of the world.

COLOPHON

Type:	Palatino and Michelangelo
Composition:	Acorn Press and Harlowe Typography
Cover page:	Strathmore Brigadoon, fife gray
Text paper:	Mohawk Superfine, softwhite, eggshell finish
Printing:	Stephenson, Inc.
Design:	John Michael